Wise Words and Sillies

A Collection of Poems

by

Susan Roome

British Library Cataloguing in Publication Data.

A catalogue record for this book is available from the British Library.

ISBN 978 0 86071 909 0

Published on behalf of the Author by

MOORLEYS
Print, Design & Publishing
info@moorleys.co.uk · www.moorleys.co.uk

Just Being Me

I know the notion of lotions and potions
To make me look younger, slimmer and thinner
Enhance my bust – pump up my lips
Whilst decreasing the size of my waist and my hips

Hair so perfect, shiny and glossy
To wear hanging loose, in a plait or a bun, ponytail,
French pleat – deciding the style is so much fun

Not allowed to cry with sadness or laughter
My perfectly made-up face would alter
Foundation ridges mascara rivers
Skin blotchy and itchy
I'm having a session, learning a lesson
To be make-up free
I'm just being me!

My Son

Hello – has anybody seen my son?
Cannot imagine where he has gone.
You'd know him if you saw him,
Eyes like melting chocolate,
Dimples when he smiles.
He's such a loving little boy,
He's brought us such tremendous joy.

We have to meet at the railway station.
No one knows our destination,
Gossips say we are going to the labour camps.
Here we go pushed up the ramp onto the waiting wagon,
No food, no water no air.
Do we have to pay a fare?
Has anybody seen my son?
Cannot imagine where he has gone.

It's his birthday next week,
He'll be turning five.
Papa has made him a little car of scraps of wood and card,
Keeping it secret has been very hard,
I have it hidden in my pocket –
I just wonder where he is.

We have travelled for days,
Covered many a mile,
No longer noticing the stench of excrement and urine in the
corner of the wagon,
And your throat full up with bile.

The train has stopped, the doors are opened,
Oh! the sweet smell of fresh air,
We are herded through the gates,
Separated into queues – men to the left,
Women to the right
And children in the middle straight.

No one is ashamed that we are all stripped naked,
We will get clean clothes when we come out of the bath house.
I tried to keep hold of the little car but I will get it back tomorrow.

Oh look over there to the left, my son, my son!
Oh! God is good, I have found where he has gone.
The children go to the bath house first
And for one second he turns his head;
Our eyes meet and the dimples are there
And then he is gone in to the bath house.

My son was black,
My son was Roma,
My son was disabled,
My son was a Jew.

*

Looking for Tock

It has stood in my granddad's hallway
For a hundred years and more,
The pendulum swinging rhythmically, tick tock
A comfort to us all.
It has withstood many a battle,
And a couple of world wars,
But one day it developed a bit of a rattle
Granddad was determined to find the cause.
The pendulum swung as normal
It was the soul of the clock,
The tick was as vibrant as ever
But it seemed to have lost its tock.
Granddad decided it needed a clean
And opened the back of the clock,
"By the time I have took out the innards
I might just discover the tock!"
The kitchen table was covered
With wheels, cogs and springs.
"I'm going to have to find a tin
To soak these parts in paraffin.
I can't afford Esso blue so cheap pink Aladdin will have to do
And whilst they're soaking we'll have a brew".
The innards had been soaking for ages,
They came out all sparkly and clean.
Granddad seemed to be well pleased,
"This is the cleanest they've ever been".
Beads of sweat appeared on granddad's brow
As the innards he started to assemble.
But by the time he had finished with the cogs, springs and wheels
The clock works it didn't resemble!
He took it all apart again,

I've an idea he started to worry.
So, trying to cheer him up a bit,
I ordered us a curry.
"This has really got me beat",
Said granddad stifling a yawn.
"I'll try to get a good night's sleep
It might look better in the morn".
We were both up bright and early,
But granddad was still feeling down
And thinking it would cheer him up,
I suggested a trip into town.
Our first stop was at the Co-op
Where granddad explained our trouble.
"I don't think the answer is here", said the assistant.
And that made another burst to the bubble.
"However", said the assistant, running a finger through her hair.
"Go to the end of the High Street, there's a man who does clock
repairs there".
We hurried off to the High Street
To get to the clock repair shop.
Our feet barely touching the ground,
Granddad was so out of breath,
I thought he was going to flop.
Granddad explained to the repair man
How his clock had lost its tock.
You'll never guess the repair man's solution.
"What you need is a bit of old sock".
The repair man drew a neat diagram
Of the innards of granddad's clock
And tidily labelled the pieces
And where to put the old sock.

We hurried home full of high hopes,
Granddad found a bit of old sock
Carefully putting it in to position,
We both stood there ears a-listening.
Did we believe it? We couldn't believe it,
The old clock had started to tock.
"Eureka!" cried granddad, running around the room,
Jumping and doing high kicks.
"But listen to it granddad, the tock is fine
But it seems to have lost its tick!".

The Whistle

Listen out for the whistle lads,
We might have a penalty kick.
Listen out for the whistle mates
It's time to be clocking out.
Listen out for the whistle crew,
An officer's come aboard.
Listen out for the whistle,
Quick the train is pulling out.

Listen out for the whistle lads,
It's time to go over the top.
Do not listen to the screams you will hear,
You haven't got time to stop.
Do not listen to the whistle of bullets whizzing past your head,
Just keep running, running, running.
If you don't you'll end up dead.
Listen out for the whistle lads,
Your time to charge has come,
Do not listen to the agonised cries
Of men whimpering for their mum.

Listen out for the whistle lads,
Three blasts and you can return.
Return to the ditch and the stench of the trench,
And the mustard gas that burns.

Listen out for the whistle boys,
Let's up and at 'em go,
Come on now, get your bayonet fixed
Come on don't stop the flow.

Listen out for the whistle,
Get your heads up over the brow,
Oh! God I think that I've been shot
Who'll blow the whistle now?

Listen to the whistle as the bugle mournfully plays,
For a lost generation never to know their halcyon days,
Listen out for the whistle.

Guy

Hello, my name is Guy, I'm part of a gang,
Who will make parliament go up with a bang,
I am in charge of the gunpowder.
There's thirty-six barrels all told,
I cannot afford to work any louder
Or our secret is sure to be told.

We know a visit to Westminster is planned
By the monarch, King James.
Our plan is to blow the place sky-high
To stop this man's cruel games.
He promised that when he came to the throne

That Catholics he would protect.
But this man's heart is made out of stone
Especially when we try to object.

And now OUR night is upon us,
November the fifth is the date,
My hands are shaking as I light the fuse,
Was that the creak of the gate?

Suddenly the cavern is full of MPs
And with the king's special guard,
One of them puts out the smouldering fuse,
One throws me in to the yard.

Kicks, thumps and punches are rained on my head,
I cannot protect myself,
Somebody shouts, "take him to the tower",
I know I'm as good as dead!

News of my capture has spread far and wide,
Luckily my friends have escaped,
All of this torture hasn't dented my pride,
My name in history is placed!

And so as we celebrate Bonfire Night
Or Guy Fawkes if you will,
Is it because at least somebody tried
Or that we have a monarchy/parliament still?

Henry VIII

Today I am the king of the land,
This is a list of things to be banned.
Cars will not be parked on the pavement,
Cyclists to the road will be sent.
"Stars" and "celebrities" banned from the air waves,
All the hot air that this move will save
Can inflate the balloon owned by my mate Dave.
We'll travel to Cheddar to look at the caves.
Countryman, lastly, I have to raise taxes
To pay "my man" to hone his axes,
I'm sorry if you think that you are badly done to
But wait 'til Mad Mary's in charge of you.

Damson in Distress

I am a damson in distress
I know I must avoid the press,
Which would turn me in to jam or jelly
Just to feed some hungry belly.

The chances of rescue are looking quite slim,
I don't want to rely on a wish or a whim,
It won't be a knight on a dashing white charger,
He's down the Dew Drop downing his lager.

I've managed to drop down on to the floor,
With a bit of a wriggle I'm under the door,
Down the path – across the meadow,
On and on to the bustling hedgerow.

Who is this come to greet me?
Hello Mr Blackbird golden beak wide open
Oh surely he's not going to…

Stay Awhile

Stay awhile, don't drive straight through,
See what Stapleford can offer you,
High Street names there are a few
Independent traders too.

Fancy a spot of history?
Stay awhile and come and see
The birthplaces of Sir John Warren, Arthur Mee
And Walter Parker VC.

Let's travel a mile out to the east
And let your eyes take in this feast,
Of monolithic sandstone rock standing fifty feet,
Sculptured by time, wind and rain,
The Hemlock stone is the name
Stay awhile, take in the view
Take a photograph or two.

Now let's return to the town
And look at the jewel in the crown,
In Saint Helen's churchyard standing proud,
Underneath the bobbing bough,
Although it may be green with moss,
There's no mistaking the Saxon Cross.
Stay awhile.

Ugo

A mystery I want solving
Before I fall off my perch,
Will not need oodles of money
And very little research.

This thing that has been my torment
From halcyon days of my youth,
Has never been explained to me
But now I want the truth.

I have questioned the minds of others,
People both haughty and naughty,
But please! Can someone explain to me
Where does the "U" go in forty?

Dog Walking

It's said a dog is man's best friend,
Some people swear this is true,
Something to fill an empty space,
Something to come home to,
Something you have to get up for,
To see that he's watered and fed,
And all that he will ask of you
Is to provide a haven – a bed.
But I wish my best friend could talk to me
Especially when we come back from the park.
I know he's trying to converse with me,
I can tell by tone of his bark.
The question I want him to answer
Before the chance has expired,
Because he has four legs, after a walk
Is he half or twice as tired?

The Invitation

There it lay on the doormat,
I could tell it wasn't a bill,
It came in a cool blue envelope,
The memory is with me still.

Wasn't quite sure what to do really,
Should I open it straight away,
Or leave it lonely, on the door mat
And look at another day?

Curiosity reared its ugly head,
Tore at the envelope, made quite a mess,
On no! It's a party invitation
What's more it will be fancy dress.

Well the imagination ran riot,
Could I go as a vicar and tart,
Or maybe a fairy tale character,
But could I pull off the part?

What about an animal?
A parrot, a monkey a cat,
This is starting to do my head
Should have left it on the mat.

I'm going to put it out of my mind
And think of something more jolly,
Perhaps I could go as a chocolate bar (or the effects of one)
Or even a strawberry lolly.

How could one small envelope
Cause such a fuss and ado?
I suppose I could say I'm busy that night
But would that be the right thing to do?

I now have three possibilities,
A pixie, a fairy an elf,
But I'm just going to buy a plank of wood,
And say I've come as myshelf!

Too Old

I'm too old to try to lose weight, I am over sixty,
Give it a try.
I'm not as nifty as when I was fifty,
Give it a try.
I'm not as naughty as when I was forty,
Give it a try.
I was quite flirty when I was thirty,
Give it a try.
When I was twenty spare weight I had, plenty,
Give it a try,
I have lost ten pounds.
I am so proud I shout it out loud,
I gave it a try!

Monkey Knit 1

Help me I'm locked in the attic
A monkey so sad and forlorn,
Make me from wool – not elastic,
Please! Let me see my first dawn.
I won't be bragging and boastful
I promise to be a good boy,
And so I remain ever hopeful.
Hey! I could be your cat's favourite toy...
So please let me out of the attic,
No one deserves such an end.
And really it's rather quite tragic
When I could be your bestest friend.

The Monkey 2

I can't believe it I'm rescued,
Out of the attic so drear.
I cannot exactly describe my mood,
But my heart is full of good cheer.
You know when those needles began to click
With wool coloured light brown and cream,
I really thought that I would be sick,
But I've excelled my own wildest dreams.
So don't give up hope all you knit kits
Covered in cobwebs and dust.
I'm living proof you can make it
And so in your owner just trust.

Wrong Shape

I am the wrong shape to wear trousers
Or even a slinky top.
I tend not to wear sparkly things in my hair
Which most times resembles a mop.
Knee length boots are a no-go,
Ankle boots are ok.
But oh my goodness what a relief
To kick them off at the end of the day.

I thought I'd try to improve my shape
And join the leisure centre,
But as people were calling me Moby,
The staff, well, they wouldn't let me enter.

But every dog has its day
And I have had the last laugh.
I've got myself a well-paid job
Down at the Greasy Spoon caff.
I won't be waiting on tables,
I'm not serving coffee or tea.
But at lunch time the place is packed to the rafters,
Everyone come to see me.
I am the lunch time stripper,
Some people say I'm "the one".
But as soon as I start my sexy dance
With one voice they all shout
"KEEP THEM ON".

The Teddy Bears' Picnic

The Teddies were having a picnic
In the college garden,
Grandma bear made a jelly
But, alas! It wouldn't harden.

She wrapped a cloth around it
And walked along the street,
Hoping she would get advice
From the people she might meet.

As she walked along the road,
She came across a wall,
A smart young man was sitting there
She could tell he wasn't tall.

"Excuse me, sir" she called to him.
"A favour I must ask,
How can I get this jelly to set
It seems an impossible task?"
"Well now ma'am", the boy replied.
"It's really hard to call,
Because at any minute
I'll be falling off this wall.
I do recall my mother
Would insert a stone cold spoon,
But that was only on the days the cow jumped over the moon".

Grandma bear turned away,
Behind her such a clatter.
The boy had fallen off the wall
And turned himself to batter!

Grandma started on her way
She climbed a steepish hill,
At the top she found the house
That belonged to Jack and Jill.

Jill answered the knock on the door,
And Grandma was taken aback
When Jill began to explain to her
What had happened to brother Jack.
"And now he's up there in his bed
It's really such a caper
Trying to mend his damaged head
With vinegar and brown paper!"

Grandma started on her way,
"Just a minute" shouted Jill.
"I don't know if this will work
But why not try a chill pill?"
"But where would I get one?" Grandma asked.
"You could try our doctor – Foster".
"I'm not so sure", said Grandma bear.
"Besides he's gone to Gloucester".

Grandma continued on her way,
She walked along the lane.
She came across two bags of wool
For the master and the dame.

Grandma mumbled to herself,
"There's something not quite right,
I'll get the little boy his wool
Though it may cause a fight".

She walked into the farmyard
Dodging around the cattle,
Thinking the boy had been deceived
She was ready to do battle.

"Are you the master of this place?"
She asked a tall young man.
"Cos I'm here to see that Johnny gets his wool
And I'll help him all I can!"

"Hold your horses there my dear",
The master said to Grandma.
"I've paid Johnny all he's owed
And he's bought himself a car".
Grandma didn't know w what to do,
She felt her cheeks aflame,
"I can't apologise enough",
Then behind her stood the dame.

"We've had to let the poor boy go
And now he has a new master,
He only earned a penny a day
Because he couldn't work any faster".
"I'm so sorry", Grandma said.
"I feel a right old Nelly
Because all I wanted when I started out
Was advice on how to set my jelly".
"Is that all?" the dame inquired.
"Well why not ask the master?
He's an educated man
I'm cooking him some pasta".

Grandma went to find him
He was standing on a bridge.
"All that's needed when you get home
Is to put it in the fridge".

On returning to her house
She followed his advice,
And at the picnic later on
Her jelly was set, cold and nice.

Wise Words

"Where words fail, music speaks".
Hans Christian Andersen

"Music is the colour of sound".
Anon

"Nature does not hurry, yet everything is accomplished".
Lao Tzu

"The only reason for time is so everything does not happen at once".
Albert Einstein

"Thinking: the talking of the soul with itself".
Plato

*"Logic will get you from A to B. Imagination will
take you everywhere"*.
Albert Einstein

*"Animals are such agreeable friends – they ask no questions,
they pass no criticisms"*.
George Eliot

"No act of kindness, however small, is ever wasted".
Aesop

"The first casualty of war is truth".
Senator Hiram Warren Johnson

Sillies

"Why am I surrounded by idiots?"
"So you don't stand out in the crowd".

They aren't making twelve inch rules any longer

"Have you ever had your eyes checked?"
"No, they've always been green".

Due to a strike at the meteorological office, there will be no weather for the next forty eight hours.

Local scarecrow honoured for being outstanding in his field.

The Experiment

The thrum of the aircraft's engine
Hung heavily on the summer morning air,
The cargo already loaded,
Unusual unique and rare.

A north-west course was plotted
To keep the plane on course,
Hiroshima the destination
The crew from the US air force.

Death, devastation, destruction
Came to Hiroshima that day,
They called the bomb "Little Boy"
In the hold of the "Enola Gay".

A stunning mushroom cloud appeared,
People rushed out to see the pall,
They weren't to know poisonous radiation
Would be the downfall of them all.

No surrender came that day,
Japan fought on and on,
So the experiment moved to Nagasaki
With another atomic bomb.

This aeroplane was called "Backspar"
The deadly cargo "Facman",
Nagasaki razed to the ground,
No discrimination in the killing,
Be it child, woman or man.
A white flag of surrender flew over the ruptured country,
The experiment deemed a success,
But was it truly reported in the world wide press?

The instigators of the experiment celebrated
with fine wine and cigars,
Never once thinking of the country their actions had scarred.
Shame on you Mr Truman,
Shame on you Monsieur de Gaulle
Shame on you Mr Churchill
Shame on you, shame on you all.